MAXIMIZE MEETINGS

IDEA-RICH TIPS ON HOSTING A SUCCESSFUL MEETING, TRAINING SESSION OR CONFERENCE

BOB 'IDEA MAN' HOOEY,
Author of Legacy of Leadership

Updated and expanded for 2024

Table of Contents

As we begin…

"All who have accomplished great things have had a great aim, have fixed their gaze on a goal which is high, one which sometimes seemed impossible…" Orison Swett Marden

Tired of sitting through ineffective, ill prepared, poorly led, and **BORING meetings?** Perhaps you find yourself taking the lead in a meeting or conference. Maximize your meetings and personal effectiveness by pre-planning and streamlining agendas.

In this book, we will take the time to discuss what makes a good meeting, training session or conference, and what characteristics you need to be an effective meeting planner or chairman. We will touch on some of the basics of good planning and parliamentary procedure. Further we will explore how to set up and conduct productive meetings by pre-planning and asking the right questions.

"Nothing gives a person so much advantage over another as to remain always cool and unruffled under all circumstances." Thomas Jefferson

Thomas Jefferson might have been writing about how to be an effective chairman. With his hand in the drafting and signing of the document that has defined our neighbor to the south he certainly understood what it took to wade through the differences of opinion, style, and personal agendas to get the job done. And so will you after you have completed this book.

I have drawn from personal and professional experience in attending, participating; and leading business, association board meetings and AGMs, as well as conducting, planning, and leading conferences and convention planning teams across North America. I have used my platform experience of working with meeting planners on 6 continents as a speaker, facilitator, emcee, panel host and panelist, and as corporate and association trainer and breakout seminar leader.

I share with you some of the fruits and lessons of those labors, in hopes, that I may give you a foundation upon which to see SUCCESSFUL, MAXIMIZED MEETINGS, because of yours.

There are many factors that influence and impact the success of any venture. Hosting a successful meeting, training session, or conference takes planning, people, and performance. If you invest the time in reading and applying what I have shared here, your event will be more successful.

Bob 'Idea Man' Hooey

You may not meet 100% Satisfaction (few meetings do so), but you will go a long way in creating and delivering an event that meets or exceeds the needs of those who attend.

This publication is derived from nearly 30 years in the meetings industry as a speaker, presenter, board member, conference chair, organizing or committee chair roles. I've kept it simple, so it is relatively easy to understand and apply.

View Bob live in these video clips

Global Speakers Summit 2013 Vancouver where Bob created and hosted an international fund-raising evening:
https://youtu.be/EqAfczlVMIg

Bob keynoting in Paris **https://youtu.be/TOKnOc4D98w**

Bob keynoting in Cape Town, SA
https://youtu.be/283cWmKFXVE

How to avoid training mistakes

As a meeting planner, you make decisions to engage or contract on programs and policies that will either help your team or hinder your team in reaching their goals.

Meeting planners can avoid making training mistakes by thinking about a few ideas and side-stepping some mistakes that have minimized returns on their training dollars. Unfortunately, training dollars are wasted because leaders make the following mistakes.

- **Failing to fully assess team needs.**
  Perhaps you are teaching your team skills they already have? Team members don't need training 'just for the sake of training.' I've heard managers say, "Even if they know this stuff – a refresher won't hurt them?"

  Sometimes that is true (I've been asked back to reinforce a program or to provide add-on or follow up sessions) – but often it can be counter-productive or de-motivating, if not handled correctly.

  Here's a suggestion: before you launch any training program, conduct a needs assessment with your team. Work to establish a comprehensive list of current team members' skills. This way you may discover what they already know, and what they need (and hopefully want) to learn. Then, as you provide training, it will send a positive message that you value their contributions and are dedicated to helping them increase and hone their skills.

- **Thinking that training sessions will eliminate conflict.**
  Often managers think that training, especially training that focuses on team or relationship building, will help eliminate conflict on the job. Some programs over emphasize 'teamwork' at the expense of **team effectiveness**. All team efforts need to be focused and task and relationship oriented.

When sessions focus too much on relationship building vs. team effectiveness, they dilute their impact, and can often become counter-productive.

Here's a suggestion: work to ensure everyone on your team knows that conflict is an important part of the team process. Without some conflict and honest difference of opinion you get mediocrity; as someone once told me "The opposite of conflict is apathy, not peace and harmony."

The secret is in not taking conflict as a personal issue, or a negative result in the process. Creative conflict can be a part of a positive process in making sure your team makes the best choice and fully explores all the options and potential pitfalls.

- **Thinking of training as a program vs. a process.** One of the challenges in training is the expectation that a half-day, full-day, or even a few days of training can change years of habit. Research shows that shorter sessions spread over a longer time result in better retention and long-range effectiveness. **Short and often** rather than a one-time massive attack seems to work best.

Here's a suggestion: for your training to be effective, insights and ideas gained must be quickly translated into action (Ideas At Work!) – actions that are reinforced by the leaders on your team. Real development is never completed, as is the true essence of education.

In my on-site sessions, I challenge my audience members to make a commitment to act on what they learn, and to schedule those actions.

I hope these suggestions will help you as you search out the most effective training programs for your team. I'd be happy to share some other thoughts with you if you have any other questions or queries. bhooey@mcsnet.ca

Meetings, boy, do we have meetings!

"A committee is a group of men who individually can do nothing, but collectively can meet, and decide that nothing can be done." **Alfred E. Smith**

Someone jokingly said, **"Thank God, when He decided the save the world… that He didn't send a committee."**

This may seem a bit harsh; but in effectively using our time, we may find our commitments to **'meeting-itis'** to be a huge time waster.

Am I saying getting together or serving on committees in a waste of time? NO, in fact, the most effective use of our time is by working together to tackle the larger goals we would never accomplish alone.

For example, the **National Kitchen and Bath Association** and its Chapters stand as a testament to the positive side of meetings.

The **National Speakers Association**, the **Canadian Association of Professional Speakers,** or our **Global Speakers Federation** are concrete examples of professionals banding together to help each other achieve more than they ever could as individuals. I'm sure you could share other examples of groups where the meetings are dynamic, informative, and valuable. **Rotary International** for example.

Join a **Toastmasters Club** and experience first-hand the value of group dynamics and encouragement in your personal and professional growth. Visit: **www.Toastmasters.org**

What I am saying is that having a meeting for the sake of having a meeting or a committee for that purpose is counterproductive. Know **"why"** you are meeting and schedule it to be tight and effective.

I have come away from countless meetings frustrated and feeling like my time has been stolen. It doesn't have to be so! Here are a few of the reasons why we have **"useless"** meetings:

- To provide an audience for someone "important"
- To socialize
- To escape from being effective
- Habit (we've always had this meeting)
- To pass the buck (easier than making a decision) or to procrastinate
- To fool people into believing they are participating in important decisions

Can you think of any other reasons?

If you become aware that these reasons exist, find a way to excuse yourself and go back to work! quietly or unobtrusively Hint: Having yourself paged or called to the phone works! It makes an easy exit and can be pre-arranged with a co-worker or assistant to give you this option.

There are **"good reasons"** where meetings work better as an effective method of communication

- Share knowledge
- Establish common goals
- Gain commitment and support from a larger group
- Provide group identity
- Team formation and interaction
- Status forum (part of the in crowd of decision makers)

Perhaps you might have a few ideas on why meetings would be a good idea?

But how do we keep our meetings effective?

Here are some fundamentals I've learned over the years from my countless corporate, community, and association meetings, about the essence of successful meetings.

- **NEED:** Hold only those meetings for which you see a clearly **demonstrated need**. If you can cover the points by memo, email, fax, or by a call or two, then don't call a meeting.

Call a meeting only when you have a problem or task that requires the input and on-site assistance of a larger group. Meetings work best when you need to gather to solve problems that are complex, exchange technical material, or explain policies and procedures that affect a great number of people.

What is the real reason or need for the meeting?

If you have trouble outlining a real need for a meeting, then I'd suggest not calling one. Your time and the time of your associates or volunteers is too valuable to squander on needless meetings. Call them wisely, based on need, and they will be much more productive.

- **PURPOSE**: Each meeting must have a clearly defined object and purpose! Those coming must know in advance what these are. This allows them to be able to prepare and bring any materials that will help the group in reaching or fulfilling this purpose.

Can you state in writing a valid well-defined purpose for this meeting? As above, if a well-defined purpose for the meeting can't be articulated, don't have it!

- **PARTICIPANTS:** Invite ONLY those people who can really contribute or have a need to know. The length of a meeting extends in direct proportion to the number of people in attendance **"who have to comment"** on the points at hand.

Who needs to be at this meeting? Why?

Many years ago, I had the opportunity to help establish the first two Home Depot stores in BC. At one of our stores, we had managers meetings, which ran conservatively twice the needed length. Our store manager would announce new policies or decisions and then allow everyone around the table to comment on them. With 35-40 managers, you can imagine our meetings ran unproductively long. I found this to be counter-productive to both my productivity and my performance and led to being one of the reasons I chose to leave this company.

- **AGENDAS:** Pre-circulated Agendas are an absolute if you wish to be effective with your meetings. Try to circulate the agenda 48 to 72 hours before the meeting, so attendees are prepared and ready to contribute. If all else fails write the agenda on the whiteboard or flip chart for last-minute meetings.

Over 75% of meetings have no pre-planned agenda. Any wonder why most of them are ineffective? Agendas 'force' the leader to focus and organize their thoughts and allocate sufficient time for each item. **Accountability works!**

Have you prepared an agenda? What items need to be on it?

- **MEETING PLACE:** Work at finding a good location with good ventilation, comfort, equipment, and proper accessibility. Ensure meeting places are free from distractions and interruptions. This is even more important if the purpose of your meeting is to brainstorm or generate creative ideas.

Do you have a place in mind that would be conducive to a productive meeting? Where might you meet?

- **PUNCTUALITY – START AND FINISH ON TIME:** This sends a clear signal to participants that their time is valued, and they are expected to respect the meeting time.

Some suggest starting with a brief uncomplicated activity so late comers can catch up.

Don't recap for those who arrive late. They will learn to show up on time, more so, if they must work at getting the information. Reward the behavior you want – **punctuality!**

- **STICK TO THE AGENDA:** Encourage participation but make a note and hold over new issues (unless they are more important than the reason you decided to call the meeting) to another meeting. Don't let the meeting get sidetracked. Keep it on track! As meeting leader this is your focus!

If you are to make a change, poll the attendees first, to see if that is their wish. Agendas are in effect a "contract" with those who attend. **Treat both with respect!**

- **LEAD A BALANCED, CONTROLLED DISCUSSION:** As the meeting leader you can 'support members' in expressing their concerns and views, even on volatile or touchy subjects; but steer away from arguments. And don't let one person 'dominate' or manipulate a meeting.

- **SUMMARIZE AND DISTRIBUTE MINUTES**: Recap the decisions and actions planned because of the meeting and circulate to those who attended.

Make sure they know who is to do what, and by when. Time deadlines and action plans are very effective. Note any follow-up or new items for the next meeting.

Effective meetings can leverage your time and help, by giving you the forum to share your ideas and gain the support you need to succeed in your life and career.

Choose carefully, participate fully, and evaluate your continued involvement, constantly.

Remember:

- **Never** write a letter, when a memo or email will do.

- **Never** write a memo, when a phone call will do.

- **Never** call a meeting when a quick visit or call can accomplish the same results.

- **Never** call a meeting unless it's the most effective means to accomplish your goals.

If you value your time and the time of others, meetings will be **"magic"** and motivating.

Bob, keynoting the PSA South Africa annual convention held in Cape Town, South Africa

Finding the time for training...

Continual training and professional development will give your team the opportunity to fully realize their potential. It pays big dividends on better-equipped, energized team players on the job.

Finding time for your team to attend training can be a challenge for most organizations. Applying some creativity to your training program can yield powerful results.

Here are a few ideas to reduce classroom time, without jeopardizing the process of quality training:

- Schedule team members to attend training between 10 am and 3 pm, instead of a full day. In this case, they can still attend to urgent business. This works well for on-site training or training held very close to your operation.

- Weekend seminars are increasing in popularity. Remember, if you ask your team to sacrifice their private time, be sure to include some group outing or banquet to show your appreciation. Trade-off time during the week may be nice too!

- Suggest your team study up on the course material in advance so they can hit the seminar running. We can provide some advanced materials to facilitate this process.

- How about scheduling a "lunch and learn" or "breakfast briefing" by inviting in a local expert when your team needs information on a simple topic. Or combine a "breakfast briefing" for management or specific team members in addition to half day or full day training.

Other ideas might come to mind that help meet your training needs more creatively? Share them with us: bhooey@mcsnet.ca

When and where to meet...

Essentially meetings fall into two categories: formal and informal. Each has its values and guidelines to being successful or effective.

Here are a few examples of **informal meetings** that you might recognize and apply:

- **Impromptu meetings:** are great on short notice to discuss issues frankly, and to reach decisions quickly without the input of large groups or attendees.
- **Small informal meetings:** are useful for discussing, problem-solving and giving feedback. They are planned so preparation is required but action can be implemented because of the smaller numbers.
- **Brainstorming sessions:** are great to generate new ideas or elicit quick ideas for solutions to situational problems.
- **Stand up meetings:** or meetings-on-the-run can be a very effective form of decision making, problem solving, and information sharing and gathering. Taking the initiative and seeking out others who need to give input allows you to get in quickly, share relevant information and make a quick decision.

Formal meetings:
- **Board meetings:** attended by the board of directors of a company or association on a regular basis to discuss business or items for the good of the group. Reports to the membership.
- **Standing committee:** is a subgroup of a company or association board given responsibilities for recurring tasks or delegated tasks. Reports back to the board.
- **Ad hoc committee:** an association or company board may strike up an ad hoc committee to study or deal with a specific issue needing attention. Reports back to the board.
- **Public meetings:** open to everyone. Used by local government or private action groups to consult the public on various issues. Sometimes used by companies wanting to

discuss developments or other changes which might affect the public in a specific area or region.

- **Conference:** offers the opportunity for a variety of presentations to be given. May also form the basis for AGM or other meeting necessary for good of group.

- **External meetings:** might be two groups meeting to negotiate such as a trade – union negotiation. Confidentiality is more important in this case and meetings are normally held on more neutral ground. May have a facilitator or mediator to allow for frank discussion and control meeting time and agenda.

- **Annual General Meetings:** often mandatory on a yearly basis for companies and associations to conduct business, elect boards, report to members and shareholders, discuss business and activities during current year and for upcoming year. Advanced notice must be given.

- **Extraordinary General Meetings:** a meeting called at any time between AGM's if member or shareholder approval is needed for immediate action. Notice must be given.

Being aware of the purposes of various meetings will allow you to prepare yourself and conduct yourself accordingly. It will also help to determine whether the meeting is on focus or not.

Check out these online resources to enhance your next meeting. There is some great information online now.

Check out this article on ideas for your next event. Why not surprise them? **www.eventmanagerblog.com/event-ideas**

Check out this piece on 80 unique & quirky corporate event ideas that your team will love. **www.coburgbanks.co.uk/blog/friday-funnies/corporate-event-ideas**

Here are some team-building-event ideas: **https://blog.bizzabo.com/team-building-event-ideas**

At the call of the Chair… tips and techniques

Why have a chair anyway? Is it important to have someone chairing a meeting? I'm sure, based on some of the meetings you've sat through that the chairman wasn't really an asset.

Having chaired a fair number of meetings in my life, I understand just how hard it is to do the job properly. I do, however, understand the importance of having someone who can keep their eyes on the objective skillfully lead a group of people through an agenda to conclusions, commitments, and positive action on those commitments.

Whether you are in a formal meeting or an informal gathering, a chairman can exert tremendous influence on the outcome. Every meeting needs a chairman to direct the proceedings. A chair is the person selected to oversee the smooth running of a meeting. They have the authority to regulate the meeting and the responsibility to enforce any rules that govern the proceedings, keep order, and act to successfully complete the business.

The Chair has the added challenge of maintaining neutrality throughout the meeting while ensuring that all attendees make contributions, listening to the views of others, blocking any negative tactics used, summarizing views and decisions, restating motions clearly, being firm with awkward people, and keeping to agenda and agreed upon time.

I'd suggest getting a pocket guide of **Robert's Rules** or some other parliamentary procedure manual as a reference to effectively doing this job. Your group should agree in advance to which one to follow in conducting your meetings.

Here are a few skills that will help you if you choose to take on this role. Brush up on these essential skills before you embark on the seas of chairmanship.

- **Firmness and dedication** to running meetings to time schedule and effectively and quickly dealing with any problems that crop up. Remember you are in charge!
- **Ability to listen** carefully and summarize relevant points succinctly.
- **Flexibility** is a great tool, especially when you must deal with different styles and tones and demands of those in attendance.
- Being **open and receptive** when listening (neutrally) to opinions you don't share, and to drawing people out so that those opinions can be fully heard, explored, and considered.
- A marked degree of **fair-mindedness** that ensures that all views are aired and given equal consideration. Sometimes this is the hardest skill to hone.

In addition, please keep in mind these following points or guides:

- As chair you are responsible for ensuring that any discussion is relevant to the points on the agenda and the items on the table for discussion. Keep them focused and on track.
- As chair you are responsible for keeping order and to expel anyone who continually disrupts the meeting. You are chosen by the whole to protect the individual, while allowing the whole to conduct business in a reasonable fashion.
- As chair you are responsible to repeat or restate any motion proposed by those attending to ensure that everyone in attendance has heard it and understood it prior to voting. You can have people put long motions in writing. You can also draw on the skills of your recording secretary to ensure you have a proper motion or amendment to restate.
- As chair you are responsible for summing up the discussion and go over the action points at the end of the meeting.

A few more suggestions:

- As chair, I'd suggest opening the meeting with a short summary of the meeting's purpose and its agenda. You might even revisit the group's vision and mission statements and have

them in plain view to assist those in attendance in keeping
focused.

- As chair, remember to allow all parties to express their views
  on each item or subject under discussion. You will, on
  occasion, need to draw out some of those in attendance, and
  hold back those who would like to talk repeatedly.

- As chair, one of the biggest challenges is preventing or
  minimizing irrelevant debate and reining in rambling
  discussions. You need to help them keep on track, focus, and
  on time.

- One other challenge is to keeps side discussions and talking to
  a minimum.

- As chair you are responsible for ensuring that any voting
  procedure is followed correctly. If parliamentary procedure
  isn't your expertise and you have someone well versed in these
  skills, you can appoint them as your parliamentarian and seek
  their guidance when needed. I did that specifically when I was
  Governor for BC's 191 clubs. It helped!

- Depending on your rules, as Chair, you may be called upon to
  cast the deciding vote. Check your organization's rules of order
  and procedures in advance of the meeting.

- Pacing a meeting is important. A suggestion might be to
  summarize actions to date and remind people how much time
  is left on allotted time for additional agenda items.

- If time runs over, suggest postponing some items for another
  time. Seek guidance from those you guide on what items they
  want to discuss. Remind them if there are time sensitive or
  deadline-based decisions that must be made. As chair, your job
  is to keep your eye on the big picture and the major goals as set
  by your group.

Being chair is not as easy as some would have you to believe. It is,
however, a very important role in your group's effectiveness and
ability to work as a team to achieve common goals and objectives.

Remember you are not there to make them ALL happy. In fact, if
you do your job well, you will at times make many of them

unhappy – when they don't get their own way. But, if you do your job effectively, your group will achieve its goals on time and as a team. It's worth the effort.

For more information check your library or online for a book on parliamentary procedure. Visit your closest bookstore and get your own pocket guide. It may prove to be an invaluable investment for you and your career.

A Creativity Break for Your Team…

Finding a way to move your team away from their established routines can work wonders in unleashing their creativity and restore their on-the-job energy.

I recall a story from Hewlett-Packard, which well illustrates this premise. Seems one morning many members of a Hewlett-Packard team came into work to discover 'subpoenas' at their desks. They had been summoned to do 'jury duty' instead of their normal routine. Hewlett-Packard executives planned a full two-day 'trial' to involve them (as a cross section of their employee base) in deciding the fate of its new business plan.

Employees were divided into three teams: one team argued against the plan, playing the role of prosecutors; one team acted as defense attorneys in its defense; and the third group was sworn in as jury. After each side had presented its case and argued the merits of their position, the jury rendered its verdict. All the employees involved in this unique event returned to their 'normal' jobs energized and excited about the company's new direction.

What kind of event can you plan to jolt your employees and team out of their routine? Does this example give you some ideas that might work in your case?

Accountability – key to effective meetings

How often have you sat in meetings listening to excuse after excuse from people who didn't do what they said they'd do at the last meeting? Does it bug you too? It does me!

One of the items I use personally to counteract this frustration, is an **action list** which summarizes what was agreed to be done, by who and by when. This action list, if kept and circulated to all in attendance immediately following the meeting, makes people more accountable for their actions and inactions. **Two things will happen**: they will start doing more; or they will stop talking and over-committing. Either way you win!

This action list (tool) can be a most effective one, if used properly and publicly. Just as in the secret of success teams, group accountability can push us to 'actually' complete that to which we commit.

If the reason for the meeting is important and vital to the success, growth or other purposes of your organization or group – don't you think the follow-through is just as important?

This is even more important in volunteer groups where people come together under a common banner with individual agendas and the challenge is to blend those agendas to the common good. Having done that, I will follow through and accomplish what has been talked about.

Don't be afraid to hold people accountable and set a higher standard. They will respond or they will leave you to accomplish what is important. Either way, you win!

Checklists and Questions
Hosting a successful meeting, training session or conference

Hosting a successful meeting, training session or convention is based on knowing in advance and taking care of the details. Whether you are planning a small board meeting, a Toastmasters meeting, sales meeting, AGM, training session, seminar, workshop, or a full-blown multi-day convention, you'll find the following questions valuable. Asking them in advance prevents someone asking you why you didn't later!

My special thanks to my fellow professional speakers and trainers in CAPS and NSA, most especially my friends from NSA-Arizona for *priming the pump* with the basics. I have edited and added a few of my own based on extensive 'learning curves' drawn from my real experiences (some expensive. ☹)

Pay attention to pre-planning and covering the details and the meeting will run more smoothly. I challenge you to have a meeting plan and a definite agenda; having the answers to the following questions, *where applicable*, will make a major difference in your success. It will make a *big difference* in the experience and effectiveness of your meeting in meeting and exceeding the needs of those who attend.

A dozen years ago, I was preparing for two days of extensive training with Executive and Administrative Assistants in BC. We discovered that they, like many association directors and meeting planners, are responsible for scheduling and planning for meetings, training sessions, conventions, and conferences. So, we covered some ideas to equip and assist them in this challenging process.

That was an interesting discovery for me, as I have had a few clients who assigned this responsibility to a junior or new member of the team. Over the years, I'd found myself coaching them and gently asking questions that helped them cover the basics in creating and completing successful training sessions, meetings, and even conferences.

The following year, I was asked to keynote for CSAE. In preparation for their annual CSAE All Alberta Tradeshow, I pulled together meeting and planning material to provide as additional resources for use when doing a meeting outside your group, for training sessions or even a conference. **"Hosting a SUCCESSFUL meeting, training session or conference..."** was born!

Someone asked me a couple of years back how many meetings I had been involved in...? I did a quick tally and was amazed to discover I'd been involved in various capacities in over 350 meetings over the past 7 years. Either as a keynote speaker, breakout or concurrent presenter, sales and management training sessions, association professional training, leadership training with some of North America's top leaders including Canada's 50 Best Managed Companies, as well as being a consultant to other meeting planners, chairing and planning committees. As well, as the program or educational director on two conferences. (One national and one inter-provincial.) Wow! No wonder I'm tired!

I've included some very valuable *questions* based on organizing, participating and speaking at several hundred such events over the years, including our annual National Speakers Association workshop, I helped host in Hawaii.

Along the way, I have had the privilege of presenting at meetings, conferences and doing training in 24 countries, so far. So, I am still learning, and will keep adding new lessons and tips as we go forward.

I share them with you as my gift to you and your potential members and clients. I hope they prove valuable, and that your meetings and conferences will be more successful, generate better attendance, and have your guests leave with some good solid ideas to apply when they return to their normal endeavors.

GENERAL OR MEETING PROFILES

- Meeting dates?

- Can dates be changed to provide negotiation flexibility?

- What are the best ways to open and close?

- Sites of other conventions or meetings - Is there any feedback that might affect this year's choice? Will you need more than one hotel?

- Budget considerations or restrictions?

- Transportation supplied for attendees?

- Group fares - are they available?

- Travel agent necessary or available to help attendees?

- Ground transportation - arranged or included?

- What is the total projected attendance?

- Will spouses attend? What have you got planned for them?

- Break down attendance by day/function as necessary?

- How many suites and rooms required?

- How many will you guarantee?

- Hospitality suites? Offices? VIP accommodations?

- Will you control all room reservations?

- Should rooms be located together in blocks?

- How do you handle the hotel bills?

- What should happen as a direct result of this meeting?

- What do your attendees expect from this meeting

- Are they a homogeneous group with much in common? What?

- How much do they know already about the proposed topics?

- Will you have general sessions only?

- Small groups/general session combination?

- Workshops?

- Seminars?

- Speakers/facilitators/MC planned and booked?

- Will there be Q&A periods?

- **What audio-visuals will be required for each meeting?**

  - Flip charts?

  - Whiteboards?

  - Floor lectern?

  - Computer linked LCD projector?

  - Video recorder or Video/DVD player?

- Any unusual audio-visual requirements?

- Will presentation(s) be audio or video recorded? (Discuss rights with speakers. Signed agreement for recording, distribution, or archive rights?)

- List meeting requirements for each day?

- Are exhibits planned?

- Trade show along with meeting? Will you need a separate area for them?

- Copy facilities available? (covering last minute changes or speaker needs)

- Secure room/area required?

- Signs?

- Security guards necessary?

- Secretarial services needed?

- Telephone message center required?

- Photographer required? How many days? Who will instruct the photographer on picture needs?

- Will you ship materials to headquarters hotel?

- Registration facilities needed?

- Registration procedures established?

- Registration personnel to be recruited hired and trained?

- Badges - designed or stock? Ordered?

- Should badges identify categories of registrants?

- How will conference or meeting be promoted?

- Is a mailing schedule established?

- Local papers and media identified and contacted?

- Will local or national press be invited?

- Insurance needs to be considered?

- What *traditional* social events should be considered?

- Opening reception?

- Awards Presentation?

- Closing banquet?

- President's or board reception?

- Emcee for any of above?

- Spouse tours?

- Plant or store tours?

- Greeting by local dignitaries?

- How much *free time* is planned for attendees?

- Are they encouraged to stay longer or come in ahead of meeting?

- Does this count in your room rates tracking?

- What are their recreational preferences?

- Golf, tennis, walking/aerobics, water sports, sightseeing, theaters/nightclubs?

- Unrestricted sessions important?

- How are breakfasts traditionally served?

- Are coffee breaks supplied?

- Special diets required?

- What function bar facilities will be needed?

- Many individual cocktail parties?

- How many will visit in-hotel lounges/nightclubs?

- Can hotel shops expect heavy patronage?

- What follow up is planned after the meeting or conference?

- Other

SITE INSPECTION

- Does the city actively solicit meeting and convention business?

- What is the public's attitude towards conventions?

- Is there a convention bureau? What services do they offer? (Indicate charges, if any?)

- Publicity campaign?

- Promotion mailings?

- On-site press relations help?

- Planning assistance?

- Registration personnel?

- Bulletin typewriters or laptop/printers?

- Bonded cashiers?

- Hosts/hostesses?

- Interpreters?

- Designation meeting coordinators?

- House bureau?

- Tour coordinators?

- What materials are available? (Indicate charges, if any.)

- B&W photos? Color photos? Transparencies? Brochures?

- City guides? City maps? Badges? Specialty items? Banners? Posters?

- Which airlines serve the local airport?

- Direct service to how many cities?

- If service is concentrated within certain hours, indicate?

- Could these times affect meeting hours?

- Distance from airport to meeting place (time and fares)?

- Schedules and charges for limousine service?

- Is airport transportation system well organized?

- Problems which affect meeting attendees in transit?

- Would airport maps help? Can you get them? (Indicate charge, if applicable)

- Is convenient public transportation available?

- Which car rental companies have airport counters?

- Are sufficient porters on duty?

- What are the rush hours for local traffic?

- Total first-class rooms convenient for meetings or convention?

- Are hotel groups in specific areas of town?

- New facilities with planned opening, prior to meeting dates?

- Is there a sales tax? Room Tax? Value added tax?

- Distance between main hotel and other facilities?

- Will charter bus service or shuttles be necessary?

- Distance between main hotel and prime attractions?

- Is public transportation safe and dependable? (indicate charges, if applicable)

- Any special cars or buses?

- Is a multi-hotel convention possible?

- Will the local auditorium fit your needs?

- What are the rental fees, rooms and capabilities?

- Is there a municipal exhibit center?

- Net exhibit space?

- Are there meeting rooms available there?

- What are the fees, capabilities and available services?

- What are the move-in and move-out regulations, fees?

- Is lighting and ventilation adequate?

- Local labor problems affecting meetings?

- Rate local exhibit service firms?

- Are local A/V suppliers professional and reliable?

- Is rental equipment up to your standards?

- Can you get names and addresses for references?

- What recreational facilities are accessible to attendees?

- Tennis courts (locations and fees)?

- Golf courses (locations and fees)?

- Jogging paths (locations and fees)?

- What is the area's general security status?

- Any specific areas to be avoided?

- How do prices compare to last year's site?

- Holidays or special local events to help promote meetings?

- What local attractions are appropriate for attendees?

- Which are the best-known restaurants?

- Which restaurants would match attendees' preferences?

- Which are the most convenient to meeting hotels?

- Are menus available?

- Hometown *talent* you can incorporate into meeting or entertainment?

- Are interesting factories or institutions open for tours?

- Names and references for tour operators?

- Shopping areas of interest to your group?

- Local union regulations or unrest to consider?

HOTEL PROFILE

- Distance from airport and driving time?

- Direct transportation between the hotel and the airport?

- List the same information for trains or buses, if applicable?

- Does the hotel have on-premises parking facilities?

- Capacities and rates?

- Are airline offices in or near the hotel?

- Are car rental offices convenient?

- What is the total number of rooms?

- How many singles, doubles, and suites will the hotel commit?

- How many smoking and non-smoking rooms?

- What cable channels are standard on in-room TVs?

- Hi-speed or computer access in rooms?

- Computer or business center access in hotel?

- What is the general level of housekeeping?

- Are hallways and public rooms clean and neat?

- Are public washrooms clean and well equipped?

- Is room service up to your attendee's standards?

- Are front desk personnel polite, efficient and helpful?

- Rate attitude and personal appearance of bell persons?

- Speedy elevator service? Large enough for your needs?

- Any bottleneck periods which could affect your meeting?

- Rate bedrooms for cleanliness and furnishings?

- Can the hotel guarantee room rates? How far out?

- Any physical changes planned for the hotel? When?

- Are copies of the changes and plans available?

- Which unions have contracts for the hotel?

- Which regulations might affect your meeting?

- Other events before, during or after your sessions?

- Will hotel inform you, as meetings are booked around you?

- Hotel policy on hotel staff briefings by meeting planners?

- Will hotel supply copies of relevant staff memos?

- How long has the General Manager been with the hotel?

- Sales Manager?

- Convention services manager?

- What was the last position he or she held? Where?

- Policies on credit cards, direct billing and check cashing?

- Security available for materials and attendees?

- Will hotel supply extension numbers and duty hours of key meeting support people?

- Check hotel's projection screens for condition?

- What audio-visual equipment does the hotel own?

- Rate each for condition and dependability.

- Does the hotel recommend outside suppliers? (Why?)

- Is the person in charge of hotel in-house equipment a repairperson, also?

- Hotel charges for using their on-site equipment?

- Any special regulations for film projections?

- What is the total number of meeting rooms which can be made available? (Capacity of each room?)

- Are floor plans available for each room?

- How accurate are advertised room capacities to practical seating requirements?

- What registration desk equipment is available? (Indicate which is free or fee) Where will it be located?

- Hotel's preferred method for handling reservations?

- How do they track accounting against guarantees?

- Does the hotel offer free registration cards?

- How far out will hotel commit rooms?

- When must guarantees be reconfirmed?

- Are advance room deposits required? How many nights?

- What is the hotel policy on late arrivals?

- Is there a penalty for early checkouts? Late checkouts?

- How are the complementary rooms allotted?

- What variables affect rates?

- Are special rooms available for convention headquarters?

- Can private phone lines and internet connections be brought into the office?

- When must final menus be submitted?

- When are guarantees required?

- What guarantees and taxes apply to food functions?

- Does the hotel offer room service?

- What are the hours and capacities for restaurants?

- What are the hours and capacities for public lounges and bars?

- Any unusual theme restaurants or lounges?

- Does the hotel have its own entertainment, nightclub or dancing area?

- Is there a package room and what is its operating hours?

- What sports facilities are on the premises? Others nearby?

- Is there a drug store in the hotel? A beauty salon? Shoeshine?

- List other shops in the hotel or adjacent?

WORKING WITH SPEAKERS, TRAINERS AND PRESENTERS

- What type of speakers – informative, humorous, and inspirational – will you consider?

- Will you need speakers, trainers/seminar leaders, or both?

- Will you need facilitators for breakfasts/feedback sessions?

- Will you need panel leaders, participants or emcees?

- What results do you want as result of the speaker's presentation?

Take time to give this specific thought so you can convey this to prospective presenters.

- Do you want a free speaker, sponsored or a fee speaker?

- Have you set an overall budget for speakers, expenses, and materials?

- Have you called NSA/CAPS/GSF or Bob 'Idea Man' Hooey for suggestions or advice?

- Will you frame your invitation early, to include: Reason for invitation? Subject of the speech? Purpose of the meeting? Meeting agenda? Audience size, age, educational level, gender? Topic and time allotted to the individual speaker. Question & Answer or discussion period to follow? Site of the meeting? Discussion of honorarium and expenses you'll cover.

- Will you be able to meet with speakers personally?

- Are tapes, CD/DVDs or copies of speeches or presentations being made available?

- Have you worked out copyright, royalties, and other legal arrangements with speakers if their sessions are to be recorded?

- If accepted, will you follow up immediately, confirming date, place, time?

- Determine special equipment, if any, required by speakers?

- Obtain biography, photograph, and introduction for speakers?

- Discover whether spouse will accompany speaker?

- Schedule rehearsals for coaching, if necessary?

- When will payments be made? By whom?

- Do all parties (Conference team and speakers) clearly understand financial arrangements?

- Will flowers or fruit be provided?

- Check for speaker's needs before the meeting?

- Have speakers been invited to pre-meeting activities?

- Determine special staging, A/V needs or props?

- Will you clear publicity releases with speaker? Can Speaker make them available to you for use in promotions?

- Get written permission (covering royalties, copyright, distribution, and fees) in advance to tape outside speakers?

- If necessity dictates a 'budget' speaker, have you considered some of these alternatives: Interview by "Reporter"? Panel discussion headed by your speaker? Question and answer sessions? Videotaped speech instead of live?

- Does the speaker know the names and professional details of other speakers?

- Will the speaker get badge and meeting kit on arrival?

- Will spouse or partner be entertained, transported, fed while speaker is working?

- Informed of any last-minute changes?

- Audio-visuals and staging; if any, set up and checked out? Is speaker's backdrop checked for distractions – mirrors, lights, doors, etc.?

- Is the stage to be cleared of any other speakers or dignitaries prior to presentation?

- All dishes and clatter to be stilled during dinner or meal speech?

- Will you take measures to fill rows down front?

- Will you save seats down front for head table during speech?

- Is there a timepiece of some sort visible to the speaker?

- Are water jugs and a glass EASILY REACHED?

- Is there tissue easily reached?

- Will all slides, charts and visuals be set up and checked in advance?

- Will you have a stage assistant, if necessary?

- Will the speaker be having items available for purchase?

- Will you provide a resource table assistant, if necessary?

- Have you cleared your introductions with the speakers?

- Will someone escort the speaker to the event or their speaking room?

- Have speakers been introduced to other participants?

- Does the speaker understand everyone else's role at that session?

- Is there an 'emergency' hot-seat speaker or fill-in program ready?

- If giving speaker a gift, have you considered its size? Can you ship it to their home or office? (Many speakers are traveling to other presentations, and it's difficult to carry additional bulky or fragile items.)

- Have local dignitaries been invited?

- Have they been provided tickets or passes for all scheduled events?

- Has local transportation been provided, if necessary?

- Informal 'welcoming committee' to await guests?

- Will you stick to the introduction agreed upon, verbatim?

- Will you keep the meeting and discussion within agreed time limits?

- Will you pay the honorarium or balance of fee before the speech? (Normal requirement)

- Will you pay the agreed expenses promptly?

- Will there be forms for audience feedback?

- Write speaker a letter of appreciation?

- If there was publicity or write-ups, will you send speaker copies?
- Will attendee comments or summaries be forwarded to the speaker?

- Is there a formal evaluation of the speech planned?

A/V AND STAGING REQUIREMENTS

- What does basic rental include? What are the extra charges?

- Available for rehearsals?

- Can equipment and materials be locked securely?

- Delivery facilities adequate? Maximum door size in length, height and width?

- Loading dock? Height? Maximum elevator size?

- What are local fire regulations? Must plans be filed with Underwriters? Fees? Liability insurance required?

- Are all workers unionized? One union?

- Any union regulations worth noting?

- Any sales tax?

- Are the available floor plans accurate? All accounted for in net space?

- Can entrance doors be located behind the audience in room set up?

- Where are the doors? Emergency exits? Pillars? Center aisles? Cross aisles?

- Re-measured to check dimensions and obstructions? Ceilings sufficiently high? Reflecting mirrors? Hanging chandeliers? (Sightlines and seating)

- Can room be totally darkened for projection? Dimmed?

- Checkroom facilities nearby? Staffed?

- Room large enough to minimize crowding? Small enough to fill? Individual temperature controls in the room?

- Accessible? Air conditioning sounds a problem?

- Telephone in the room? Can it be turned off?

- Phone jack or Internet connection in the room? Will it be live?

- Distracting noises outside the building?

- Percentage of permanent seating? Temporary?

- Is temporary house seating comfortable?

- How many square feet per person when set up?

- Wide enough for your set up? With enough power?

- Are circuit breakers conveniently located?

- Platforms needed for projectors. What size?

- Room behind the audience to set up platforms?

- Will projectors be level with screen center?

- Are there room dividers?
- Are sliding walls *really* soundproof?

- If not, what will be happening in adjacent room during meeting?

- Is there a permanent stage? Height from floor? Depth, height, and width suitable?

- Are there wings or rear areas for performers awaiting cues?

- Temporary staging available? What size platforms? Stage steps available? What size? How many?

- Standard runway (36" high, 42" wide) sufficient?

- Bandstand needed?

- Stage curtains that open and close? Motorized?

- Stage lighting sufficient?

- In-house supplementary lighting available?

- Draping colors/room decor compatible with presentation? Draping for stage required? For runways? For tables?

- Cherry picker or double ladder available for high work?

- PA/sound system adequate? Make? Wattage?

- High or low impedance? How many mikes provided free? Possible interference for wireless mikes? Where are the speakers located? Sound mixer available?

- Sound tech necessary? Can one be on call?

- Spotlights available? Operators necessary?

- Sufficient outlets? Additional outlets available?

- Permanent screen? Matte? Beaded? Color? Size? Height from floor? Front projection? Rear projection?

- Portable screen in good condition?

- What equipment is in-house? (List wattage, brand and condition)

- Slide projector (indicate slide size) Extra trays or carousels available?

- LCD projector for computer visuals

- Extra screens (list sizes)

- Whiteboards

- Electric pointers

- Flipcharts and easels

- Recording sound equipment

- Video recorders and players. Format? CD/DVD players

- TV/VCR (List sizes)

- Is there an in-house audiovisual supplier?

- Theatrical/House electrician's rates?

- Includes benefit payments and any applicable taxes

- Overtime? Minimums? Call outs?

A note from Bob

If you've taken the time to read through this exhaustive (I'm sure we've missed a few ☺) list of questions, by now your head is swimming. And you haven't even gotten the answers to all of them.

Realistically, **not all these questions are applicable for your event**. It does; however, make sense to see which ones do, and to make sure you and your planning team have done your homework in answering them. The answers to these questions and process to getting them will provide you and your team with a **workable guideline or solid foundation** on which to successfully build and create your event.

I'd be happy to assist you in this process. I offer planning advice and consulting as well as my being available in speaking, training or facilitation roles. Over the years, I have found myself coaching inexperienced or new meeting planners through the process.
I have developed a whole series of downloadable checklists, tips and techniques in addition to recommendations for other resources for this purpose. I invite you to visit my **www.ideaman.net** site to learn more about my motivational keynotes and innovative training sessions.

I wish you and your team all the success! I'd love to be a part of your event success team.

Someone once told me the secret to a successful meeting is in the details. I have developed a fairly comprehensive checklist that covers the majority of pertinent questions you might want to ask in order to ensure you've covered everything.

Visit www.ideaman.net/MeetingPlanners.html for a downloadable series of detailed, downloadable, free checklists and links to additional on-line resources.

Budget Planning Guide – watch your financials

Attention to details in all aspects of your planning process builds solid foundations for success in the eventual outcome of the event. Knowing the base line **fixed costs** and the potential additional costs in advance will allow you and your team to plan effectively and deliver a well-run, **profitable**, and enjoyable event.

- How much money do you have to work with? Do you have a preliminary allocation or budget figure to work with? Do you have a copy of last year's event budget numbers?
- Who approves the budget? Who is involved in working out the details? Who do you need to talk with to get additional information or estimates for inclusion?
- Is your event expected to break even or provide a profit for your organization?
- Who handles the payments, and how are they to be processed?
- Will you design your budget to be flexible in reaction to attendance figures and additional, unexpected costs?

The following list is laid out as a reminder of some of the typical areas in a meeting, training session or conference. The more you detail in advance, the better your event, and the less chance of unpleasant budgetary surprises later.

My suggestion would be to use this as a planning tool to cover all the fixed and potential budget costs.

Then, after consideration of projected attendance and revenues adjust it accordingly. Often, I have designed my events with a base line break-even budget and added or upgraded accordingly when certain attendance or revenue figures are reached. This allows your team to plan and yet be flexible in providing more value for those who attend, if revenue is available.

REVENUE:

- Registration fees (*members*) $ _________
- Registration fees (*non-members*) $ _________
- Registration fees (*partner, staff*) $ _________
- Event fees (*partial attendance*) $ _________
- Sponsorships (*breaks, food, etc.*) $ _________
- Resource table and on-site sales $ _________
- Advertising (*Program, materials*) $ _________
- Organizational budget contribution $ _________
- Other (*e.g. auction, 50/50, shirt sales*) $ _________
- Other $ _________

TOTAL PROJECTED REVENUE: $ _________

EXPENSES:

SITE SELECTION:
__ Conference planning meetings $ _____
__ Design committee meetings $ _____
__ Pre-meeting travel $ _____
__ Site inspection expenses $ _____
                    Sub-total: $ _________

HOTEL EXPENSES:
__ Exhibit Halls $ _____
__ General session rooms $ _____
__ Meal function rooms $ _____
__ On-site office/event staff $ _____
__ Board meeting room $ _____
__ Hospitality room(s) $ _____
__ Press room $ _____
__ Officer/Director rooms $ _____
__ Special guest suite(s) $ _____
__ Speaker/presenter room(s) $ _____
__ Speakers preparatory room $ _____
                    Sub-total: $ _________

FOOD:

__ Meals *(itemize)* $ _______
__ Refreshment Breaks *(itemize)* $ _______
__ Breakfasts $ _______
__ Banquets $ _______
__ Luncheons $ _______
__ Dine-around buffets $ _______
__ Receptions *(itemize)* $ _______
__ Cocktail parties *(itemize)* $ _______
__ Board meetings *(itemize)* $ _______
__ Committee meetings *(itemize)* $ _______
__ Hors D'oeuvers $ _______
__ Other *(itemize)* $ _______

Sub-total: $ _________

PRESENTERS, FACILITATORS:

__ Keynote, general session $ _______
__ Seminar leaders $ _______
__ Breakout/concurrent $ _______
__ MC, host, panel leader $ _______
__ Spouse program $ _______
__ Staff program $ _______

Sub-total: $ _________

ENTERTAINMENT:

___ Entertainer(s) $ _______
___ Disc Jockey $ _______
___ Piper $ _______
___ Band/improv group $ _______
___ Other $ _______

Sub-total: $ _________

Here is Bob's most recent teaser video. <u>youtu.be/-fAFD9mkUPo</u>

TRAVEL COSTS:

__ Speaker travel *(itemize)* $ _____
__ Entertainment travel *(itemize)* $ _____
__ Conference team travel *(itemize)* $ _____
__ Staff travel *(itemize)* $ _____
__ Director/officer travel *(itemize)* $ _____
__ Airline fares and taxes $ _____
__ Ground transportation $ _____
__ Taxis and limos $ _____
__ Shuttle buses $ _____
__ Porters, skycaps $ _____
__ Bell persons $ _____
__ Staff transportation $ _____
__ Departure taxes, Airport fees $ _____
__ Shipping of materials $ _____
__ Storage and handling $ _____
__ Courier and delivery $ _____
__ Special needs transportation $ _____
__ Tips and gratuities $ _____
__ Other $ _____

Sub-total: $ _________

AUDIO VISUAL:

__ Sound system $ _____
__ Portable & Lav. microphones $ _____
__ Extra speakers $ _____
__ Special lighting $ _____
__ Screens (size_______) $ _____
__ Reverse projection screens $ _____
__ LCD/LED projectors $ _____
__ Video and audio recording $ _____
__ Speaker special needs $ _____
__ Flip charts $ _____
__ White boards $ _____
__ Signage, posters $ _____
__ Pads & Pencils $ _____

Sub-total: $ _________

PERSONNEL/STAFF:

__ Outside consultant's fee(s) $ _____
__ Secretarial services $ _____
__ Clerical assistance $ _____
__ Association/organization staff $ _____
__ Courier services $ _____
__ Meeting planner assistants $ _____
__ Travel coordinators $ _____
__ Registration personnel $ _____
__ Registration desk on-site $ _____
__ Volunteer expenses $ _____
__ Drivers $ _____
__ Special A/V people $ _____
__ Video cameraman/projectionist $ _____
__ Lighting & Sound man $ _____
__ Photographer(s) $ _____
__ Carpenters & Stagehands $ _____
__ Electricians and technicians $ _____
__ Security services $ _____
__ Guards for trade show/event $ _____
__ First Aid attendant(s) $ _____
__ Legal & accounting services $ _____
__ Childcare $ _____
__ Minister $ _____
__ Tips, Gratuities $ _____

Sub-total: $ __________

GIFTS & AWARDS:

__ Recognition certificates $ _____
__ Plaques $ _____
__ Award for special guest(s) $ _____
__ Speaker plaques $ _____
__ Speaker welcome packs $ _____
__ Speaker gifts $ _____
__ Flowers for VIP's $ _____
__ President's gift $ _____
__ Director/Officer(s) gifts $ _____
__ Door prizes $ _____

___ Committee gifts $ _____
___ Committee plaques $ _____
___ Partner gifts $ _____
___ Special gift for attendees $ _____
___ Bag/briefcase for attendees $ _____
___ Speaker book for attendees $ _____
___ Winner's awards & trophies $ _____
___ Officer/director recognition $ _____
___ Certificates of participation $ _____
___ Certificates of completion $ _____
___ Other $ _____

Sub-total: $ _________

RECREATION:

___ Golf $ _____
___ Tennis $ _____
___ Outings $ _____
___ Sightseeing & excursions $ _____
___ Other $ _____

Sub-total: $ _________

MISCELLANEOUS EXPENSES:

___ Website development $ _____
___ Room Taxes $ _____
___ Sales Tax, GST $ _____
___ Personal vehicle use – mileage $ _____
___ Gratuities not already included $ _____
___ Insurance $ _____
___ Shipping & Storage $ _____
___ Overtime $ _____
___ Office supplies $ _____
___ Furniture & computer rentals $ _____
___ Telephone & fax expenses $ _____
___ Walkie Talkies $ _____
___ Shipping supplies $ _____
___ Other $ _____

Sub-total: $ _________

POST EVENT EXPENSES:
__ Thanks for attending note $ ____
__ Evaluation summary mailed
   to speakers & directors $ ____
__ Posting speaker notes to web $ ____
__ Other $ ____

Sub-total: $ ________

DECORATION:
__ Banners $ ____
__ Room signs $ ____
__ Flag rental $ ____
__ Flowers and plants $ ____
__ Center pieces/set up $ ____
__ Stage, riser set up $ ____
__ Stage backdrop/drapery $ ____
__ Stage lighting $ ____
__ Props, theme set ups $ ____
__ Other $ ____

Sub-total: $ ________

TRADE SHOW or EXHIBIT:
__ Set up on site $ ____
__ Booth back and side drapery $ ____
__ Electrical set up $ ____
__ Sound systems $ ____
__ Banners $ ____
__ Special signage $ ____
__ Table rentals $ ____
__ Lighting set up and fixtures $ ____
__ Rugs and flooring $ ____
__ Trash receptacles $ ____
__ Other $ ____

Sub-total: $ ________

PRINTING & SUPPLIES:
__ Writers $ _____
__ Graphic Design $ _____
__ Promotional pieces $ _____
__ Pre-registration forms $ _____
__ Ticket order forms $ _____
__ Sponsorship forms $ _____
__ Exhibitor forms $ _____
__ Registration packet envelopes $ _____
__ Welcoming letter $ _____
__ Registration forms $ _____
__ Session evaluation forms $ _____
__ Conference evaluation forms $ _____
__ Name badges, holders, ribbons $ _____
__ Convention program $ _____
__ Individual session programs $ _____
__ Trade show program $ _____
__ Sponsorship listings $ _____
__ Sponsorship banner $ _____
__ Postage and mailing $ _____
__ Envelopes and stationery $ _____
__ Photo processing $ _____
__ Special acknowledgements $ _____
__ Special announcements $ _____
__ Convention schedule $ _____
__ Daily agendas $ _____
__ Special meal tickets $ _____
__ Special event tickets $ _____
__ Special function tickets $ _____
__ A la carte tickets $ _____
__ Sign up forms $ _____
__ Workbooks and handouts $ _____
__ Awards dinner program $ _____
__ AGM printing $ _____
__ On-site newsletter $ _____
__ Evaluation forms $ _____

__ Banners and signs $ _____
__ List of eating places $ _____
__ List of local attractions $ _____
__ Speaker information packs $ _____
__ Speaker confirmation letters $ _____
__ Acknowledgement letters $ _____
__ Other $ _____

Sub-total: $ __________

SUMMARY:

REVENUE: $ __________
EXPENSES: ($ ________)

ESTIMATED PROFIT/(LOSS): $ _______

This is not meant to be the *"all inclusive"* budget form. It will give you some good guidelines as to the types of things you need to include when planning your next meeting, training session, or conference.

As with the checklists, some of these line items will be applicable, and some will not. Feel free to adapt this for your specific needs and requirements.

Please contact us at IDEAS AT WORK! if we can be of further assistance in your next project or event. **Check Bob's availability to facilitate, or to present at your next event.**

Bob 'Idea Man' Hooey, Accredited Speaker, Trainer, Facilitator
www.ideaman.net
www.BobHooey.training
bob@ideaman.net
1-780-736-0009

Choosing the right seating style for your event

Picking the right layout is one of the most effective ways a meeting planner can maximize their return on the investment of their members, event team and the speakers. Taking time to select and directing the hotel facility staff on the proper placement for each portion of your event, will deliver some amazing dividends.

If you don't tell the hotel or facility staff which seating placement style you want, they will simply set up the way they have been doing, which is often the easiest way. Unfortunately, that may not be the best way to utilize the talents and skills of the speakers or presenters you have engaged for this event.

Ask the speakers if they have a preference. In my case, depending on what I am doing I prefer a herringbone style seating arrangement vs. the typical theater style. This herringbone style allows for some eye contact and interaction between my audience members and gets away from them only seeing me and the heads of those in the rows ahead of them. And… it is easily set up by the facilities staff. In fact, it takes no more time to do so, regardless of what they may tell you. It is your event, make sure they set it the way you want it.

Obviously, you cannot do a set change on a breakout room for each of a series of speakers. Consult and then pick the set that makes the best overall arrangement.

Here are the nine *basic* room seating arrangements. Being able to select the proper one for each portion of your event will help the speaker. It will also earn you the *gratitude* of those who sit in the audience. It will also help you work with the staff at the venue.

Banquet style seating arrangements work in many situations.

Keep in mind if you are having speakers, that some of your members will have to turn their seats to be able to see them.

Space may be a challenge if you have a large event. If that is not a factor, then make sure you do not overload the tables.

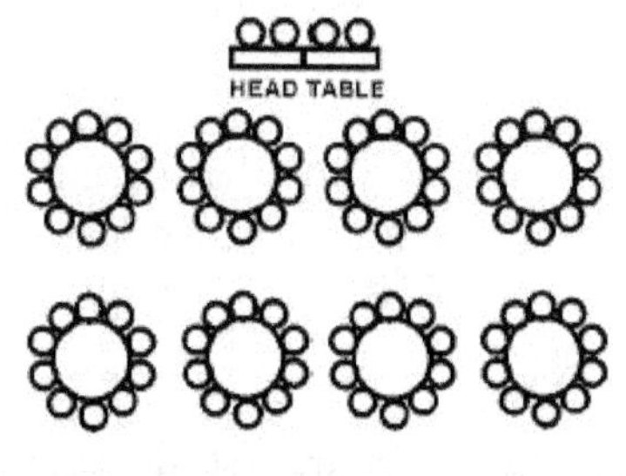

Facilities staff will squeeze as many in as possible. You want 6-8 maximum on each table! I would go for less, where possible.

In some cases, where possible you want them set so the top 2 are empty to allow for better site lines and to avoid people sitting with their backs to the speaker or having to twist to see. This can be very frustrating and painful.

If you have a smaller meal function, with a feature speaker… here is a better idea!

Again, it depends on the size of your audience and the facility you book. Pick one that best serves the needs of those who will attend.

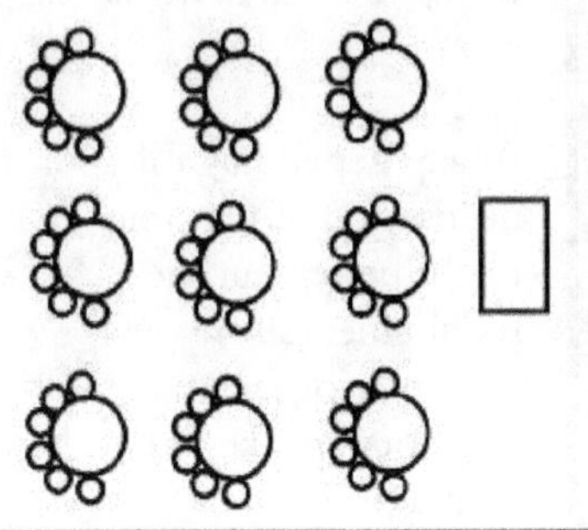

I have found this seating format to be the best for functions where the speaker or awards play a major role in the meal.

Again, let the facilities staff know exactly what you want and specify how many at each round. I'd suggest 5-6 maximum for the best effect.

I like this set up for small group work when I am training as it lends itself to interaction and real dialogue.

It also has my audience already broken into management sized mini groups.

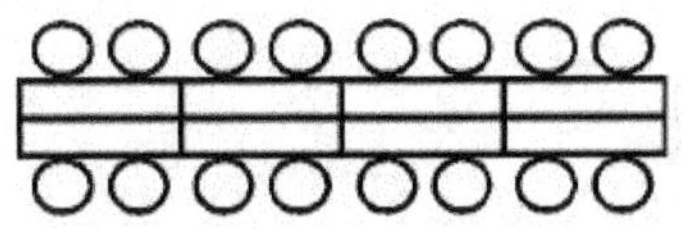

When you need a face-to-face meeting… or you want to be able to place people according to rank or position… this works.

This can work as well when you desire interaction and dialogue in smaller-sized groups.

Again, depending on your needs, one of the other styles might better suit the requirements for your presenter or facilitator.

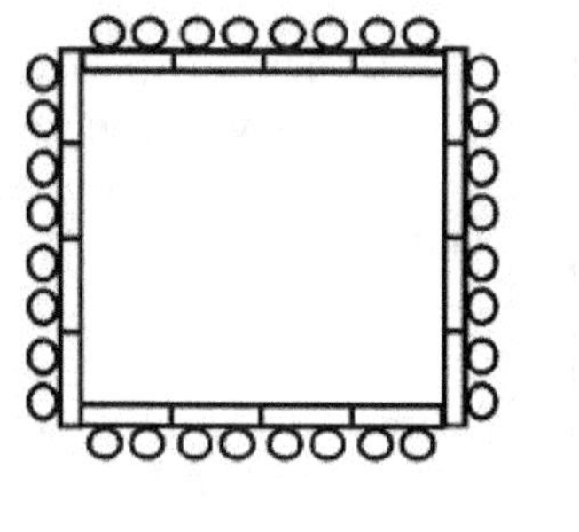

This works when you need a face-to-face meeting as well.

This can work well when you desire interaction and dialogue in medium sized groups.

Again, depending on your needs, one of the other styles might better suit the requirements for your presenter or facilitator. Ask your speaker what they would prefer!

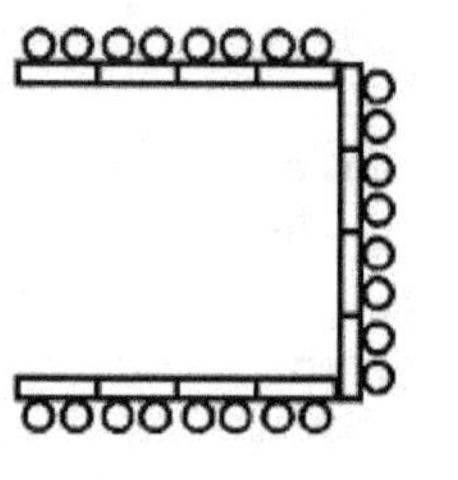

This also works when you need a face-to-face meeting or interactive training session…

This can work as well when you desire interaction and dialogue in small to medium sized groups.

Again, depending on your needs, one of the other styles might better suit the requirements for your presenter or facilitator. Ask your speaker what they would prefer!

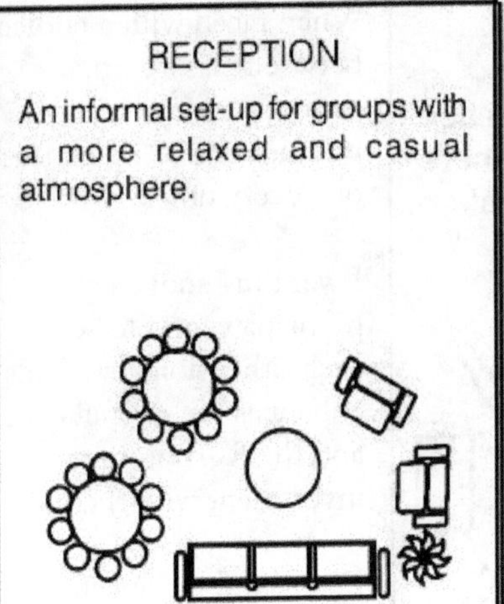

Many meeting planners are designing their events with special places where members can sit and talk to each other - White spaces for conversations.

I've found the interaction and conversations can be as valuable, or even more so than what happens in the meeting rooms.

Provide informal spaces where people can sit and share ideas and get to know each other. This will enhance your program results.

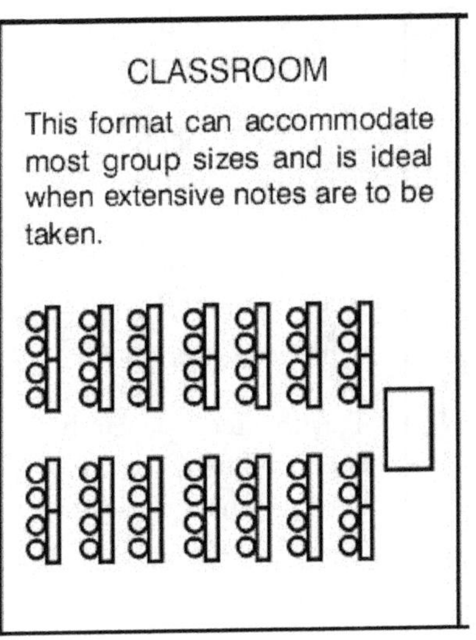

Some training programs require members to work on a table and, also, to take copious notes. In such cases, this typical classroom style set up is ideal.

It allows you to get a fair number of people in the same room to listen to a speaker or trainer as they take them through a program.

Again, ask your trainer what works best in their experience for their programs.

When faced with a choice between classroom, theater style or herringbone… I pick this one every time.

I want my audiences to participate, and to see each other doing so. This enhances the overall event and the ROI on my investment with them.

I've found facility staff to be very accommodating once I explain my reason for this choice.

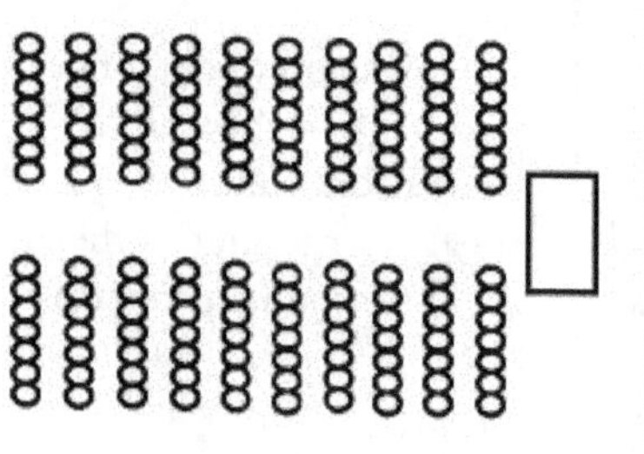

This is the more typical seating arrangement.

In fact, this will be the default choice for most facility staff unless you state otherwise. I don't recommend it if you can help it.

This theater style can be enhanced by going to a herringbone style seating arrangement.

This will allow some interaction and is more comfortable as seating allows members to sit at an angle to the speaker.

Designing a winning program, working with a planning team, recruiting the best presenters for each session, and enticing your members to attend will tax your abilities.

You will be investing a fair amount of time and money in hosting your event. Why not take that little extra time to design the placement of seating for each portion. This will allow you to maximize your investment and leverage the ROI of your speakers and members alike.

Your facility staff (catering or banquet staff) take their lead from you. If you demonstrate your commitment to hosting a well-run and well-designed event, they will respond accordingly.

Accredited Speaker, Bob Hooey presenting in Beijing, China

Meeting Planner Links and Resources

Here is a quick reference guide to some of the websites that offer practical and use-it-now information for meeting planners.

http://www.canadianspeakers.org Canada's premier site for access to professional trainers, facilitators and keynoters. Protect your investment with a professional on your team.

http://www.nsaspeaker.org USA based site of the National Speakers Association – The voice of the speaking industry. North American 'Experts' who speak.

http://www.trafficbuild.com Since 1992, corporate marketers, trade show organizers, special event planners, and publishers have benefited from our customized, turnkey promotion solutions.

http://www.ideaman.net/MeetingPlanners.html Bob 'Idea Man' Hooey has gathered use it now resources for meeting planners

http://www.specialeventsite.com Designed to serve the needs of Event Professionals, SpecialEventSite.com is an easy-to-use tool for accessing industry-specific information and for purchasing products and services over the Internet.

https://www.worldtimeserver.com/time-zones Need to make a phone call to someone far away? Need to arrange a videoconference, telephone- or net-based meeting with several people spread around the globe? This utility should help you find a convenient time, so that no one has to be up during the middle of the night.

http://www.AlbertaSpeakers.com – Information on Alberta based speakers – Gain the Alberta Advantage!

http://www.accreditedspeakers.com – Toastmasters International created this professional level designation to recognize those speakers with outstanding skills in public speaking.

http://www.corbinball.com/ The Meeting Technology Headquarters: The world's most comprehensive site about meeting planning and events technology, a REALLY great meeting technology speaker. Honoured by MPI and NSA for good reasons.

http://www.meetingnews.com The complete online source for news and information for the meeting, convention, incentive and trade show professionals. MeetingNews.com features the latest industry news, searchable article archives, crucial business resources and much more.

http://www.mpiweb.org The recently redesigned MPI Web. Deeper content and easier navigation are two new features, as well as a brand-new media centre with updated news, information and research.

http://www.pcnametag.com A great place to get all your name tags and other convention materials. Fast and reasonable. Tell them Bob sent you.

We will add additional links as we find them. These links were working as of mid-November, 2019. If you find a broken link, please let me know. If you find another good link and would like to share it with your fellow meeting planner professionals, email us: **bob@ideaman.net**

On-line resources and magazines for meeting planners

There are some great on-line and in-print magazines and other resources designed to assist the professional meeting planner or the meeting planner who just got delegated the role. I subscribe to several of these magazines and have bookmarked a few urls for my own research and resources. Check them out for yourself.

You might want to do the same, to ensure you are well-equipped to serve your members in designing and delivering a successful event.

- **http://www.successmtgs.com/successmtgs/index.jsp** – Successful meetings

- **http://www.specialevents.com/** – Special events

- **http://www.promomagazine.com/** – Promo

- **http://addall.tradepub.com/free/icp/** – Insurance conference and other publications

- **http://www.meetingsfocus.com/** – publish 4 regional meeting magazines

- **http://bpubs.tradepub.com/ brands/bpubs/cat/Mect.cat.html** – access to on-line free subscriptions to a number of magazines

These are just a few links to prime your pump.

Seven Reasons to Hire Professional Speakers

Hiring the right motivational keynote speaker, breakout, concurrent session speaker, or trainer for your company or association meeting is vital to its success. **Bring in the person who does *exactly* what you'd hoped for, and more – and people will compliment you for months.**

Of course, if you don't, you might never hear the end of it. ☺

How can you better ensure that the speaker or trainer you hire will be effective, successful for your group *and* make you look good? One good way is to look first to the professionals who are not only committed enough and qualified to become members of the **Canadian Association of Professional Speakers** or **The National Speakers Association**; but also follow the guidelines and code of ethics of that organization.

CAPS and NSA are two of the four founding members of the Global Speakers Federation for Professional Speakers, which has over 5000 professional members worldwide in 16 member organizations, as of November 2019.

Here are seven reasons why hiring *one of these pros* will benefit you and your organization:

1. A professional who earns their living speaking and training brings the kind of wide, insightful experience that will help make your sessions a success.

2. Professional speakers and trainers can supply the references, which will give you peace of mind. (There are thousands of reasons – happy clients!)

3. Professionals will give you support material that lets you know what subjects they speak on and what types of programs they

do (seminars or workshops, keynote speeches, luncheon or dinner talks, etc.).

4. Professionals will tailor their presentations to meet the needs of your event, team, or group.

5. Professionals will give you credentials, which demonstrate or indicate their commitment to the speaking profession.

6. Many professionals can give you audio (or even video) recordings that make it easier for you to judge whether they're right for your group.

As we become wired, much of this information is on-line. Check their web sites too! My primary one is **http://www.ideaman.net** ☺ You can also visit my **www.BobHooey.training** website

7. Professionals know how to set up a room to give you the best advantage and will stay within the time guidelines you require.

Hire a member of the Canadian Association of Professional Speakers, listed online at **www.canadianspeakers.org**, you'll have a better opportunity to insure you'll get a high quality, professional job. Best of all, you can rest easy knowing in advance you hired the best.

Check out NSA for US based speakers. **www.nsaspeaker.org**

Your group will be applauding you, as well as the speaker, when the presentation is over.

PS: We have 16 member organizations in the Global Speakers Federation. Check to see if there is one in your area. https://www.globalspeakersfederation.net/ Tell them I sent you. ☺

For more information on CAPS contact Bob 'Idea Man' Hooey at 780-736-0009 or email him, **bob@ideaman.net**

10 Tips for Finding the Right Speaker

Your speaker selection is one of the most important elements in hosting a successful meeting. Selecting the right speaker for your meeting can be a daunting task, as speakers are available in every fee range and specialty topic.

The **Canadian Association of Professional Speakers**, as a founding member of the Global Speakers Federation for Professional Speakers, comprised of more than 5,000 professional speakers, with 16 member organizations compiled these tips to help make your meeting, training session or conference a success.

1. **Determine the needs of your audience:**
   Thorough knowledge of the needs of your group is essential in selecting the right speaker. Does your meeting require that the audience leave with specific or technical information? Do you need someone to motivate the group to sell? Are you looking for after-dinner entertainment with a message?

2. **Establish your date, time and budget:**
- Start looking for a speaker as soon as the date for your meeting is set. Many top-level speakers book engagements up to a year in advance and you will want to get on their calendar as soon as possible.
- Consider how much time you need to fill and where that time falls in your overall program. If your time slot is flexible, a professional speaker can often tell you the right amount of time for the job. A professional can also make recommendations about the order of topics/speakers if one presentation will follow another. (You may not want to follow a humorist with a detailed or technical, educational presentation.)
- Factor in the fee you are willing or able to pay for a speaker. Your search for a speaker can be narrowed or broadened based upon your budget.

3. **Identify the type of speaker who will best match the needs of your audience:**
    A speaker's expertise in a given field may be the big draw, but a well-known name does not guarantee a professional presentation. High prices don't always mean high quality. Will your audience and the overall program benefit most from a celebrity, an expert in the field, a popular sports personality, a best-selling author, or a professional speaker who has a thorough knowledge of the appropriate topic?

4. **Locate your resources:**

-   Personal referrals are a great way to narrow your search. Ask colleagues for recommendations.

-   Speaker's bureaus locate and book speakers according to your specifications and needs. A bureau can locate speakers and quote fees. Many bureaus specialize in particular speakers such as celebrities, authors, or athletes. Speaker's bureaus can often be found in your local phone directory under "Speakers Bureau" or "Agent." You can also use the internet to find bureaus in your region.

-   Check out CAPS Online Directory of Professional Speakers at **www.canadianspeakers.org**. This directory contains information on Canadian speakers and can be searched by topic, keyword, location, name and so on. You can also check **www.nsaspeaker.org** for US based speakers. NSA and CAPS members work well together.

-   If you are outside North America, we have 15 additional professional speakers' groups in the Global Speakers Federation and more forming all the time. **www.globalspeakersfederation.net**

5. Review your options and interview your speaker candidates:

-   A professional speaker will be a *real partner* in this process. Often, they will ask questions about the needs of your audience and what they can accomplish for you. Ask your candidates for references and, if they are speaking in your area, ask if you can attend the program and observe them in action.

- Assure that a potential speaker has addressed groups similar to yours. Talk with them about their experience. Ask for a biography, testimonials, and videos of their presentations, preferably before a live audience.
- Find a speaker who will tailor his or her presentation to your group.
- Ask the speaker if they belong to professional associations. Also ask what awards or certifications they have earned.

6. Select your speaker:

- Hire a professional and you'll hire an ally. Professional speakers understand that your reputation is riding on their performance. Their experience with hundreds of audiences can add to your peace of mind and to the success of your event.
- When selecting your speaker, consider that you are not paying for the time the speaker is on the platform, but also for the hours spent researching, preparing, and customizing the presentation. Some speakers may negotiate their fees when they are doing more than one program for you or when they are allowed to sell their products. Ask about your options.

7. Get it in writing:

You should have a letter of agreement, engagement or contract that clearly outlines the expectations of both you and your speaker. Consider:

- travel arrangements and transportation;
- accommodations and meals;
- fees, reimbursements and payment terms;
- whether you want the speaker to attend social events;
- if the speaker may sell products, and if so, how this will be handled;
- an agreement on any audio or videotaping of the presentation;
- cancellation policies;

- audio/visual requirements;
- legal implications, if any, your contract may contain.

8. Work with your speaker:

Share information about your group or company. This will help the speaker become familiar with your organization, while facilitating a customized presentation.

- Send your newsletter or anything, which would include key people, buzz words or insider news and views.
- Give the speaker a clear outline of what you expect.
- Be specific about the size and demographics of your audience.
- Let the speaker know in advance about other speakers on the program. This gives the speaker the opportunity to build on (and not duplicate) what the other speakers say.

9. Set the stage:

- Make sure the room is set up for optimum impact. Consider the number of chairs and how they are arranged. Also consider room temperature and lighting.
- Stay on schedule. Although a professional will be able to "make up" time or slow things down if needed, keeping your program on schedule will allow your audience to get the full impact of the program you have created for them.
- Your speaker should be able to provide you with a good introduction of themselves and their topic. The introduction should be short, energizing and create positive expectations.

10. Evaluate the results:

Have your audience complete evaluations on the speaker and his/her presentation. This will allow you to gauge your results and plan for future programs. Send copies of the evaluations and audience feedback to your speaker.

Copyright and license notes

Maximize Meetings: Idea-rich tips to hosting a successful meeting, training session or conference

Success Publications
a division of Creativity Corner Inc.
Box 10,
Egremont, Alberta T0A 0Z0
www.successpublications.ca
Creative office: 1-780-736-0009

Acknowledgements, credits, and disclaimers

As with each of my books, a very special dedication of this piece of myself, to the two people who meant the most to me, my folks **Ron and Marge Hooey**. Sadly, both my parents left this earthly realm in 1999. I still miss our time together and your encouragement and love. I was blessed with the two of you in my life.

To my inspiring wife and professional proof-reader and publications coach, **Irene Gaudet**, who loves, encourages, and supports me in my quest to continue sharing my **Ideas At Work!** across the world. Thank you seems so inadequate for your timely work in helping make my writing and my client service better! I love the time we spend together!

My thanks to the many people who have encouraged me in my growth as a leader, speaker, and engaging trainer in each area of expertise including *Hosting a successful meeting, training session or conference.*

To my colleagues and friends in the National Speakers Association **(NSA)**, the Canadian Association of Professional Speakers **(CAPS)**, and the Global Speakers Federation **(GSF)** who continually challenge me to strive for success and increased excellence.

To my many **Toastmasters** friends and family around the world, to whom I owe an un-payable debt of gratitude for your investment, encouragement, time, and support when I was just starting down this path; and oh, so rough around the edges.

To my great audiences, fellow leaders, students, coaching clients, and readers across the globe who share their experiences and enjoyment of my work. Your positive and supportive feedback encourages me to keep working on additional programs and success publications like this updated version. My experience with you creates the foundation for additional real-life experiences I can take from the stage to the page, the classroom to the boardroom.

My thanks to a *select* few friends for your ongoing support and 'constructive' abuse. You know who you are. ☺

Bob keynoting the 2015 AFCP convention in Paris, France. He also keynoted the European Speakers Summit in Paris hosted by AFCP in 2019.

Disclaimer

© 2000-2024 ALL RIGHTS RESERVED.

No part of this book may be reproduced or transmitted in any form whatsoever, electronic, or mechanical, including photocopying, recording, or by any informational storage or retrieval system without the expressed written, dated and signed permission from the author or publisher.

LIMITS OF LIABILITY / DISCLAIMER OF WARRANTY:

The author and publisher of this book have used their best efforts in preparing this material. While every attempt has been made to verify information provided in this book, neither the author nor the publisher assumes any responsibility for any errors, omissions or inaccuracies. Graphics are royalty free or under license. Care has been taken to trace ownership of copyright material contained in this volume. The publisher will gladly receive information that will allow him to rectify any reference or credit line in subsequent editions.

Unattributed quotations are by Bob 'Idea Man' Hooey

The author and publisher make no representation or warranties with respect to the accuracy, applicability, fitness, or completeness of the contents of this program. They disclaim any warranties (expressed or implied), merchantability, or fitness for any purpose.

The author and publisher shall in no event be held liable for any loss or other damages, including but not limited to special, incidental, consequential, or other damages. As always, the advice of a competent legal, tax, accounting or other professional should be sought.

What they say about Bob 'Idea Man' Hooey

*As I travel across North America, and more recently around the globe, sharing my **Ideas At Work!,** I am fortunate to get feedback and comments from my audiences and colleagues. These comments come from people who have been touched, challenged, or simply enjoyed themselves in one of my sessions.*

I'd love to come and share some ideas with your organizations' leaders and their teams.

"I've known Bob for several years and follow his activities in business with interest. I originally met Bob when he spoke for a Rotary Leadership Institute and got to know him better when he came to Vladivostok, Russia to speak to our leadership. **When you spoke I thought you were one of us because you talked about our challenges just like yours.** *You could understand the others, which makes you a great speaker!"* **Andrey Konyushok**, *Rotary International District 2225 Governor 2012-2013, far eastern Russia*

"I still get comments from people about your presentation. **Only a few speakers have left an impression that lasts that long.** *You hit a spot with the tourism people."* **Janet Bell**, *Yukon Economic Forums*

"We greatly appreciate **the energy and effort you put into researching and adapting your keynote to make it more meaningful to our member councils.** *Early feedback from our delegates indicates that this year's convention was one of our most successful events yet, and we thank you for your contribution to this success."* **Larry Goodhope**, *Executive Director Alberta Association of Municipal Districts and Counties (retired)*

"Thank you Bob; it is **always a pleasure to see a true professional at work.** *You have made the name 'Speaker' stand out as a truism - someone who encourages people to examine their lives and make adjustments. The*

personal stories you shared with your audience made such a great impression on everyone.

The comments indicated you hit people right where it is important - in their hearts. *Each of those in your audience took away a new feeling of personal success and encouragement."* **Sherry Knight**, *Dimension Eleven Human Resources and Communications*

"Without doubt, **I have gained immeasurable self-assurance.** *Bob, your patience and your encouragement has been much appreciated.* **I strongly recommend your course to anyone looking for self-improvement and professional development."** **Jeannie Mura**, *Human Resources Chevron Canada*

"I am pleased to recommend Bob 'Idea Man' Hooey to any organization looking for a charismatic, confident speaker and seminar leader. I have seen Bob in action on several occasions, and he is ALWAYS on! Bob has the ability to grab his audience's attention and keep it. Quite simply, **if Bob is involved - your program or seminar is guaranteed to succeed."** **Maurice Laving**, *Coordinator Training and Development, London Drugs*

"I have found **Bob's attention to detail** *and his ability to fine tune his seminars to match the time frame and needs of the audience to be a valuable asset to our educational program."* **Patsy Schell**, *Executive Director Surrey Chamber of Commerce*

"Great seeing you in Cancun and congratulations on a job well done. **The seminar was a great success! Your humorous and conversational style was a tremendous asset.** *It is my sincere hope that we can be associated again at future seminars."* **Donald MacPherson**, *Attorney at Law, Phoenix, Arizona*

"What a great conference. *It was a great pleasure meeting with you at the Ritz Carlton, Cancun and I shall look forward to hopefully welcoming you and your family in Dublin, Ireland someday."* **A. Paul Ryan**, *Petronva Corporation, Dublin, Ireland*

Bob caught on stage at the 3rd annual PAPS convention in Manila. Philippines

*"Congratulations on the **Spirit of CAPS Award**. You have worked long and hard on behalf of CAPS …**helped many speakers including me** and richly deserve this award. Well done my friend."*
Peter Legge, *CSP, Hof, CPAE*

*"I had the pleasure of hearing and watching Bob Hooey deliver a keynote speech several years ago when he gave a presentation at a Toastmasters International Convention. **Bob impressed me greatly with his professionalism, energy, and ability to connect with his audience while giving them value.** I heartily recommend this talented speaker and 'Idea Man' to all who want to move to the next level."*
Dr. Dilip Abayasekara, *DTM, Accredited Speaker, Past Toastmasters International President*

*"I attended **Speaking for Success** in Edmonton. **The mark of a true leader is someone who will lay down their own pride to teach all they know to their potential successors.** To be taught by a man of his caliber was an honor whether you're a beginner like myself or a professional; the experience is well worth it! To Bob - it truly was an honor to meet you. Stay humble and enjoy the great success."* **Samantha McLeod**

Engage Bob for your leaders and their teams

"I have been so excited working with Bob Hooey, as he has given inspiration and motivation to our leadership team members. Both at the Brick Warehouse – Alberta and here at Art Van Furniture – Michigan; with his years of experience in working with business executives and his humorous and delightful packaging of his material, he makes learning with Bob a real joy. But most importantly, anyone who comes in contact with his material is the better for it."
Kim Yost, former CEO Art Van Furniture and CEO The Brick

Motivate your teams, your employees, and your leaders to 'productively' grow and 'profitably' succeed!

Protect your conference investment - leverage your training dollars.

Enhance your professional career and sell more products and services.

Equip and motivate your leaders and their teams to grow and succeed, 'even' in tough times!

Leverage your time to enhance your skills, equip your teams, and better serve your clients.

Leverage your leadership and investment of time to leave a significant legacy! **Call today** to engage best-selling author, award winning, inspirational leadership keynote speaker, leaders' success coach, and employee development trainer, **Bob 'Idea Man' Hooey** and his innovative, audience based, results-focused, **Ideas At Work!** for your next company, convention, leadership, staff, training, or association event. You'll be glad you did!

1-780-736-0009 to connect with Bob 'Idea Man' Hooey today

www.ingramcontent.com/pod-product-compliance
Lightning Source LLC
Chambersburg PA
CBHW071503030726

47593CB00003B/1128